A Taste of Leadership™
Thoughts on Leadership, Coaching, and Life

Danny Valenzuela

Associate Certified Coach (ACC)
Distinguished Toastmaster (DTM)
Certified Public Manager (CPM)
Competent Leader (CL)

DEDICATION

The dedication
　　　　of this book
　　　　　　　　is split four ways.

To my mom and dad,
　　　　who instilled my integrity and values
　　　　　　　　through how they lived their lives.

To my wife Becky,
　　　　who has stood faithfully by me
　　　　　　　　all these years, never once
　　　　　　　　　　　　uttering a discouraging word.

To my friends, who have always given me
　　　　the benefit of the doubt
　　　　　　　　and have helped me in more
　　　　　　　　　　　　ways than they will ever know.

To you, the reader,
　　　　I hope you get as much out of reading it
　　　　　　　　as I have writing it.

CONTENTS

PREFACE

I started writing a monthly newsletter almost five years ago. It was always difficult for me for a variety of reasons, but I kept at it. Over time, it became easier—not easy, but easier. I cringe when I read articles from the first couple of years. I am so grateful readers did not unsubscribe en masse. Instead, they were encouraging and always supportive.

My articles mostly focus on providing insight into leadership challenges and development. I always hope that my articles will open the reader's eyes and mind, cause them to pause and reflect, and provide encouragement.

I also hope they will share what I write with others who can benefit from my insight. If I have been able to enlighten someone, to bring quality thoughts to their process, to help in any way, no matter how slight, then I have achieved my intention.

This book is by no means the answer to all leadership questions, but is merely a taste of what I have spoken or written about during my career. I hope that somehow it touches your mind and heart.

UBUNTU, UBUNTU, UBUNTU!

Cinco de Mayo (May 5) has special meaning for individuals of Mexican heritage or with ancestral roots in Mexico. It has special significance to me because my maternal grandfather and both my paternal grandparents were born in Mexico.

Cinco de Mayo is not Mexican Independence Day, as many people think. Mexican Independence day is September 16. We celebrate Cinco de Mayo because against overwhelming odds, 4,000 Mexican soldiers defeated 8,000 French soldiers at Puebla, Mexico on May 5, 1862. Puebla is located about 100 miles east of Mexico City.

On several occasions throughout our history, Americans and Mexicans have fought bravely side by side. After the attack on Pearl Harbor during WWII, thousands of Mexicans crossed the border to join the US Armed Forces. During the Persian Gulf War, American consulates were flooded with phone calls from Mexicans who wanted to join and fight another war alongside Americans.

As effective leaders, and coaches for that matter, understanding and embracing cultural diversity is imperative. As the world gets smaller, and information moves faster, we will have the opportunity to interact with people of all races and ethnic backgrounds at some point.

Coaching in a multicultural world can be both challenging and rewarding. It can be an experience in which the coach learns as much about himself as the coachee. Understanding other cultural experiences and multicultural orientations can be valuable in guiding the client to learn from within

1

him/herself.

In the Hispanic community, it is common to greet each other with an abrazo (embrace) when we meet, and again when we depart. It replaces the handshake. I have noticed that individuals of many different nationalities now give each other an embrace upon meeting or when saying goodbye. It gives one a sense of trust, of comfort, of family.

The saying "Mi Casa es su Casa" is very popular in the Hispanic community. It translates as, "My house is your house," but literally means, "What's mine is yours." It encompasses a sense of generosity and inclusiveness—bringing joy to the person who hears it as well as the person saying it. It conveys a great generosity and willingness to share one's wealth with others.

Communities of color have their own kinship and bonding rituals. As the Latino community has the abrazo, the "high five" of the African American community is now a part of its mainstream culture— both a way of communicating and bonding.

When Native Americans meet, they share their tribal background. They do this to honor each other's ancestry and acknowledge the historical connections between tribes.

Understanding and embracing other people's cultures and traditions can add to our understanding of why people do things the way they do, and why they are sensitive to certain issues or practices that we don't understand. It places more responsibility on us, gives us more wisdom, allows for more tolerance, generates universal kinship, promotes diversity not divisiveness, makes us more generous, and enriches our lives.

Today it's Cinco de Mayo; on another day, it will be Martin Luther King Day, St. Patrick's Day, Cesar Chavez Day, or a tribute to Lori Piestewa, the first Native American woman to die in combat fighting for our country.

As leaders, as citizens, and certainly as coaches, we can only enrich our experiences, our community, and ourselves if we embrace cultural differences. It is the core of who we can be, both as individuals and as a community.

There is an African saying, "Ubuntu, ubuntu, ubuntu!" It is derived from the African Bantu language and roughly translates as, "I am what I am because of what we all are together." We are all members of this community, together.

Celebrate Cinco de Mayo with me in your own way. Enjoy the richness of celebrating not just your culture but also those of others. Embrace cultural diversity.

MEET YOUR GREMLIN

Have you met your Gremlin yet? You may not be aware or focused on it, but believe me it is always there. Your Gremlin is that narrator in your life whose sole purpose is to rob you of your vibrancy and competitiveness—in essence, to make you miserable. It is your inner-critic, negative voice, and disempowering entity. It took a while for me to acknowledge mine. For the longest time he simply took control of many aspects of my life.

A Gremlin is a maker of mischief. While I cannot verify this, it is said that members of the Royal Air Force invented the Gremlin in the 1920's. Works written in the 1940's use the term Gremlin for "an imaginary gnome-like creature that causes difficulties in aircraft." It has since taken on a life of its own and can appear in any form it desires or you acknowledge.

Gremlins are very tricky, sophisticated, and have developed elaborate methods to get in the way of our natural, excited, and vibrant soul. Once you know it is there, and how it is trying to run your life, you will appreciate its creativity.

Here are some signs that your Gremlin is around:

- You are paralyzed with indecision.
- You compare yourself to others and draw conclusions about yourself based on that comparison.
- You have done nothing or little to realize your dream.
- You feel good about yourself only if you hear it constantly from others.
- You think in terms of black and white.

- You have been in self-pity and/or victimhood too long.

Your Gremlin might be saying:

"Who do you think you are?"
"You can't do that."
"They'll find out you really don't know what you're doing."

Meet my Gremlin; he has a knack of changing his features, but I know when he is around. I named him "Firebrand" because he always tries to kindle a revolt within me. This way I acknowledge him when he appears, and I let him know I am aware that he is trying to sabotage me. I have even met some of my coaching client's Gremlins. At first, they may not be aware that they have one, but during the coaching process they usually become aware and develop the ability to visualize and deal with it.
You cannot ever really get rid of your Gremlin; you just have to acknowledge that it is there and learn not to let its chatter ruin your life. Once you acknowledge it is there, you can do some things to minimize the negative impact it can have.

In his book *Taming your Gremlin*, Rick Carson mentions three things you can do to quiet your inner critic.

Simply Notice. Do not take the chatter in your head too seriously; simply noticing it is the first step. The two important elements of simply noticing are awareness and choice.

Choose and Play with Options. Change for a change, play with different behaviors, and consider changing the behavior. Select options that are creative and that are out of character for you. You will see the value in it and enjoy what it does to tame your Gremlin.

Be in Process. While it might be unsettling, being in process is about attitude—an appreciation that your life will forever be unfolding and your future always unknown.

Taming your Gremlin can happen at any moment, with any breath. It is an ongoing process that can be challenging and exciting once you are aware and learn to appreciate your own gift of life.

SEEING WITH YOUR HEART

How many times did you "go for it," or maybe "didn't go for it" because something just didn't feel right? We do not always see everything in a clear and focused way, and even an optometrist cannot help us see it clearer. Sometimes we continue to probe an idea or action to see whether we feel we have all the information necessary to proceed.

Occasionally we have to go beyond our traditional five basic senses—listening to our "gut feeling" instead. This gut feeling is really the powerful sixth sense known as intuition. Intuition is about connecting with your heart as well as your head.

Neuroscientists have identified an enteric nervous system in the human gut, confirming that intelligence is not housed in the brain alone. These transmitters, which connect the two systems, are called peptides, and they match the brain-cell receptors. You may have experienced this when you listen to reason yet want to heed your inner voice at the same time. Doing these together is one of the challenges we face in our work and personal lives. Many times, it takes great courage to know and do things you cannot totally explain.

You probably know it as "a mother's intuition." Somehow, moms just seem to know what to do when something is wrong. Some call it a feeling, and it can appear as a pit of fear in your stomach. How you handle those intuitions, and what you do with them, can make all the difference when making a decision. Some people are not confident enough to follow their instincts. Some people will go against all odds on intuition and be right every time.

Self-trust can be harder than trusting others and yet much more valuable to cultivate. We accomplish the most by believing in ourselves and trusting our intuition.

I learned in my coach training that accessing and speaking my intuition with my clients was essential to being a great coach. One of the coaching competencies of the International Coach Federation is coaching presence. It requires the ability to be fully conscious and to create a spontaneous relationship with the client, employing a style that is open, flexible, and confident.

A sub-category of coaching presence is the coach "accesses own intuition and trusts one's inner knowing"—or "goes with the gut." When we use our intuition in coaching, we demonstrate a different way of knowing that logic and rationality cannot explain. We give ourselves permission to express what "popped up" during the coaching conversation without wasting time analyzing our thoughts and perhaps skipping over something important. Some coaches call this "dancing in the moment," letting the music (conversation) take you where your heart leads.

Where does intuition come from? In the book *Emotional EQ*, by Robert Cooper Ph.D. and Ayman Sawaf, they wrote, "In truth, all of the experiences you've acquired in your life and work are not sterile facts stacked on shelves, but are emotionally laden memories that are stored in the brain. The sum total of those experiences, your life wisdom, doesn't present itself to you as a clean, edited list of 'important things that matter' but instead as instantaneous hunches, as the sum total of gut feelings."

Intuition appears in everyday interactions of all kinds. The next time your "gut" tells you to do or say something, remember: you simply may be seeing it with your heart. If your intuition tells you it's time to think about talking to a coach to help you overcome some of the obstacles in your work or life, go for it— contact me.

Trust your intuition and it will serve you well.

LEARNING IS MORE IMPORTANT

Leadership development is the focal point of organizations today. A rapid and ever changing global environment, a desire for tangible results and understanding that people are more motivated to learn if the experience is relevant to their lives makes Action Learning **(AL)** a preferred way to develop leaders. By definition, AL is learning by doing real work. That can mean many things to many people so in this issue we try to make sense of it.

I returned from a business trip to Mexico as part of an assignment as a coach/facilitator for the Leaders across Borders **(LaB)** program. I was assigned to a team of five health professionals from the United States and Mexico who are participants in the program. The purpose is to enable them to apply new and revisited leadership skills to a real border health issue. The team consists of three health professionals from Baja California and two from San Diego.

The team's projects are designed to use an action learning approach. They select an issue important to them and reflect on what they learn. It is done in a group so that they collaborate and learn from each other. They gave their report on their project at the completion of the program.

However, the focus is not on completing the project but rather on what they learn about working across borders to solve problems. In fact, the team I am coaching has stated they will not finish their project by October but have committed to continue working together to complete it after the program has ended. The emphasis is on what they learn and that they apply that learning to continuing the program and any other projects they collaborate on in the future.

In essence, action learning is learning by doing. So many universities use some form of action learning via case studies, role-playing, and experiential analysis. Activities and feedback often form the basis of face-to-face training.

A good definition of action learning is from the book *Understanding Action Learning*, by Judy O'Neil, ED.D. and Victoria J. Marsick, Ph.D. They define it as:

> An approach to working with and developing people that uses work on an actual project or problem as the way to learn. Participants work in small groups to take action to solve their problem and learn how to learn from that action. Often a learning coach works with the group in order to help the members learn how to balance their work with the learning from that work.

Action learning coaches use many group-coaching tools when applying action learning. One that is particularly useful is the learning journal. A learning journal helps support both the task work as well as the learning of each participant. The journal is a book for recording the thoughts and feelings one experiences on the project.

One of the most difficult aspects of action learning is evaluating the program. It can be complicated to check for learning and performance gains at different levels including satisfaction with the program, immediate learning gains and those made after the program, impact of performance on the job, and impact on the organization. It is difficult to link learning to impact.

So how do we define success when using action learning? In Leaders across Borders, success is defined by the learning goals established at the start of the program. These include:

- TRANSFER OF KNOWLEDGE FROM CLASSROOM TO REAL WORK: What aspects of the of LaB classroom did the team bring to their project? Did the team try something new? Did individuals try something new? What?
- STRATEGIC RELATIONSHIPS: Did the team members create new relationships? Will these be long lasting relationships?
- KNOWLEDGE OF HEALTH SYSTEMS: Have individuals on the team increased their understanding of their own country's health system/issues and those of another country?
- HIGH PERFORMING TEAMS: Did the team increase their understanding of and/or abilities for creating and leading a high performing team? In what ways did they do this?
- UNDERSTANDING OF SELF: Did the individuals increase their own understanding of self as a leader?
- OTHER: Were individuals willing to share their knowledge and experience?

This project has been very rewarding and a terrific learning experience for me as well. I especially enjoy the bicultural and binational aspect of the program as well as the opportunity to use my bilingual skills in the practice of coaching.

It has been a great experience to see people from

both sides of the US-Mexico border work in unison to solve health issues that affect both countries.

Is your team ready for an action learning experience?

TO CHERISH OUR DESIRE WITH ANTICIPATION IS TO HOPE

We often think that our accomplishments are the result of hard work, intelligence, and sometimes luck. Many times, we do not realize that it was our original dream that gave rise to our vision and hard work to pursue that dream. People who hope are sometimes called dreamers. Leaders who help other people realize their dreams, reach their goals, and do things they sometimes did not think they could, are called "dream-makers." A critical role of leadership is to recognize the dreams of those you lead and inspire them to achieve their visions, their dreams.

The International Rescue Committee (IRC) in Phoenix recently asked me to coach three refugees who were starting a new life. The IRC helps refugees thrive in the country that gave them sanctuary and a new beginning. These individuals hope to fulfill their dreams of business ownership. I never asked why these individuals were refugees in our country; it does not matter. I only know that they hope for a better life than the one they left behind.

What was obvious to me is the desire they have to be successful. They are working hard: long hours every day, fueled by the power of belief, imagination, and will. They are hopeful of a better future, grateful for the opportunity to realize their dream and find a way out of their current dilemma.

Many of my coaching clients are trying to make a positive change in their lives, their jobs, their careers, or their businesses. Their hope is to become better leaders, better managers, better problem solvers, and the type of individual that people want to follow. It is not easy to separate our personal lives from our work lives nor do we always want to. They are interchangeable. What affects one affects the other no matter how hard we try to keep them separate. What is happening in our work environment impacts our home environment and vice versa.

My most productive work with clients is with those who are hopeful, willing, and courageous. They know they can be successful but need the skills of a coach to meet the challenges of change and the challenges of the future. I help them achieve personal excellence and business success while maintaining the integrity of their values and beliefs.

Hopeful leaders know it takes courage to turn the unbelievable into the expected. Being hopeful is being human. It is about being able to see with your heart and move forward in the face of uncertainty toward the future—to go after it and not wait for it to come to you. Hope is about learning to believe.

We cannot mistake hope for optimism. Optimists expect things to turn out well for them without any effort. Pessimists assume all is doomed and there is nothing to be done except spread despair while there is still time.

Hope is based on uncertainty because we do not know what will happen next. However, the real place for hope is in the possibility we possess for acting, changing, and mattering.

ARE YOU COMMUNICATING OR JUST TALKING?

Every day we communicate. We talk with the intent of conveying information to a person or persons. But are we getting our point across? Are there more effective ways to communicate? Ways that will enable us to get what we want out of the conversation? Being an effective communicator is a strong trait of an effective leader. We should learn to understand our communication preferences and adapt them to the different styles of those with whom we communicate.

A recent article in the *Arizona Republic* discussed the importance of determining others' communication style and then responding accordingly. The article listed some of the most common styles:

> **The Analytical**: Business like, slower-paced, time conscious and focused on facts.
> **The Driver**: Fast-paced, focused on results.
> **The Expressive**: Fast-paced, enjoys variety, big picture projects and recognition.
> **The Amiable**: Slow-paced, excellent at building relationships, listening and sharing their personal life.

So which is your style? There are many tools and processes we can use to discover our communication style and explore the preferences of others. The key is to understand our own communication preferences and take the time to discern others' communication style. If we learn to understand how others respond to us, we can adapt our communication to fit our needs at the necessary moment. The key is to stay flexible.

Knowing your subject is certainly one aspect of effective communication. Mastering communication requires knowing what to communicate and when. People possess different goals, fears, motivations, and different ways of seeing the world. If they are different from ours it does not make them wrong, yet leaders must learn how to recognize these differences and adjust their style of communication accordingly.

Becoming an effective communicator also requires a high level of self-awareness. This is essential to understanding your personal style of communicating. It will help create good and lasting impressions on others. This does not mean you have to be a chameleon, changing with every personality you meet. Instead, you can make the person listening feel more comfortable by selecting and emphasizing certain behaviors that fit within your personality and resonate with them.

In our **Ascending Leader's Program**™, participants learn ten tools and processes to become effective leaders. It equips functional managers and potential leaders with the decision-making and implementation skills they need to excel as leaders. They emerge better equipped to take on greater cross-functional responsibilities and ultimately drive performance throughout their organization.

At Transition Execs, LLC we coach our clients to meet the challenges of change and the challenges of the future, enabling them to achieve personal excellence and business success. We teach them to use their strengths as a foundation to transition their management skills and leadership style to develop into high performance individuals or teams.

THE SIX SUITCASES YOU CARRY IN LIFE

As we go through life, days turn into weeks and weeks into years. The journey takes us in one direction or another. Like most travelers, we carry suitcases with the possessions we need for our journey.

There are six suitcases that contain our essential possessions. We add contents to five of the six suitcases as we go through life. Yet the most important one is the sixth suitcase, which contains everything we need when we are born. This sixth suitcase is essential to the effective use of the contents of the other five.

I am always looking for books that contain relevant coaching information and effective coaching tools. One such book is *The Business Coaching Toolkit*, by Stephen G. Fairley and Bill Zipp. One chapter in particular talks about our sixth suitcase.

The authors identify the five suitcases we pack as we travel through life. They are:

1. The **Work** Suitcase: our achievements
2. The **School** Suitcase: our education and training
3. The **Personality** Suitcase: our temperament
4. The **Interests** Suitcase: our tastes and hobbies
5. The **Values** Suitcase: our character

However, without the sixth suitcase we cannot effectively use the contents of the other five. If we do not understand what is in our sixth suitcase, we will base our ambitions on only the first five. As a result, all our efforts may end in frustration.

When we unpack our sixth suitcase, we will find that it contains all the **natural gifts and talents we were born with**. It is this unique mix of innate strengths in each of us that allows us to excel at certain things in life.

For example, the unique individual is able to remain calm and lead in a crisis. It is the musician who composes music in his head without writing it down, and yet the result is a masterpiece. On the other hand, it could be the business owner who listens to his intuition, does something that others consider risky, and successfully brings a product to market.

We fill our first five suitcases as we go through life. We start that life with our sixth suitcase already full, but it is up to us to unlock its potential and power. It is up to us to use the natural talents in our sixth suitcase and align them with what we do in our daily life. Many times, they are so instinctive that we do not realize we have them. As a result, we focus on fixing our weaknesses instead of building on our strengths—leading to frustration and unfulfilled dreams.

Another reason why we should unpack that suitcase is that when we do not have balance in our life, we are out of alignment. When a tire is out of alignment, it wears unevenly, causing it to wear out faster than normal. When we go to work unbalanced and out of alignment, we do not do those things that come natural to us, so we tend to wear out as well. When we do not use our true talents, we are drained of energy and creativity, sometimes becoming demoralized. We are better at what we do when we use our natural talents and come to work energized and motivated.

A coach is trained to help clients unlock their sixth suitcase. Using their strengths as a foundation, I help them transition their management style and leadership skills to develop into higher performance individuals and teams.

If you or someone you know could use some assistance in unpacking the sixth suitcase, I can help. Check your alignment to see if you are wearing well, and take care.

IS IT CONFLICT OR CONSTRUCTIVE DISCONTENT?

Managing conflict in the workplace is an important leadership skill. People often think of conflict as fighting. It might be, but fighting is only one way of dealing with conflict. Conflict is the condition in which people's concerns appear to be incompatible. A concern is anything about which people care. In an organization, people's concerns might center on such things as deciding how to allocate resources, determining what facts bear on an issue, and supporting different strategies.

Having the skills to resolve conflicts in an organization or business is a major challenge faced by CEOs and business owners. People frequently mention handling conflict in a productive way as one of the most challenging skills. When setting up Standard Oil Company, the elder John D. Rockefeller said, "The ability to deal with people is as purchasable a commodity as sugar or coffee, and I will pay more for that ability than for any other under the sun."

As leaders, it's up to us to resolve conflicts. We can do it in a way that destroys productivity and relationships, or we can address it as "constructive discontent" and discover ways to approach the challenges it provides. Letting go of our comfort zone can be very difficult, and constructive discontent can help us realize when it's time to let go and try something new—to take a leap of faith.

Many of the advances we make are a result of constructive discontent. When we are unhappy about something, we get creative and come up with ways to do it different, or we invent something to make a change. The discontent becomes a source of progress.

To lead smarter is to communicate, not trying to suppress the constructive discontent but staying grounded and learning skills to deal with those emotions. We must become less stressed and develop ways of reframing our thinking that help us move past the emotions we undoubtedly will feel.

In a recent blog, Irene Becker, a coach and consultant, gives us tips to building constructive discontent. I share them with you today.

1. Expect change to be stressful, but know that you can use it to move forward smarter, faster, and happier.
2. Understand and limit crisis orientation.
3. Be gentle with yourself. Get rid of the negative self-talk.
4. Resist negativity because it will not take you forward. Develop positive habits of thought, positive coping styles that will allow you to build constructive discontent.
5. Develop habits of thought that will help you shift your perspective and discover new options.
6. Develop flexibility by simply identifying one rigid pattern of behavior/coping and turning it around.

One thing for sure is that we have to know our own conflict mode and style, and how we can adapt in conflict situations, as well as knowing the adaptive modes and methods of others around us.

Being constructively discontent may not be a bad thing if it is encouraged. Discontent with status quo and exploring avenues for growth can keep an organization and its employees hungry to accomplish more.

To quote Cornelius Jansen (1585–1638), professor at the Old University of Louvain, "An organization is a mosaic—it is the profile of many contributions. The pattern is never a singularity—it is the fitting and shaping of many pieces."

Conflict resolution is one of the modules in our **Ascending Leader's Program™.** Join me as a participant in the program and you will learn what your conflict mode is and how to identify other's modes, plus the best ways to work with them.

THINK SMALL, BE SMALL. THINK BIG, BE CONFIDENT!

Most people, at least those I know, want to be successful in their marriage and family life as well as their job. This does not take intelligence or innate habits, but it does require us to learn how to think and behave in ways that get us there. One way to do that is to build confidence and destroy the fear that holds us back. Thinking is about thinking that you are what you think you are.

In his book, *The Magic of Thinking Big,* David J. Schwartz, Ph.D. mentions numerous things we can do to achieve what we want in life. It centers on how we think and how we overcome our fears. Our thinking is what holds us back. Shakespeare once said, "There is nothing either good or bad except thinking makes it so." Success can be obtained not so much by the size of our brain, but by the size of our thinking.

For many it can start by realizing the excuses we make for not accomplishing what we want. Schwartz calls it "Excusitis." A sign of excusitis is when someone presents numerous reasons when explaining why his or her plans have not worked out. We can call this the "why" syndrome: why they did not, why they cannot, why they do not, why they are not. Successful people do not make all these excuses.

One of the keys to overcoming excusitis is never to underestimate yourself and your intelligence. Make sure you remind yourself regularly that your attitudes are important. Develop and create ideas and better ways of doing things, and your age (younger or older) will not be a factor. You are not too old, nor too young, to open the doors of opportunity.

One way to win confidence is to determine what is holding you back and then take action. Use your brain as a depository of positive thoughts. Deposit only positive thoughts in your memory bank. Deposit those little victories or positive things you saw today. Count your blessings and be thankful for your wife, your children, your health, your friends, or whatever it might be.

Every night before you go to sleep, deposit those positive thoughts in your memory bank. When the time comes to withdraw thoughts from your memory bank, withdraw only positive thoughts. Negative thoughts only ferment in your mind and destroy your confidence.

Effective leadership requires us to THINK BIG. Schwartz gives us four leadership principles to work on.

1. Trade minds with the people you want to influence. Before you act, ask yourself this question: "What would I think of this, if I exchanged places with the other person?"

2. Apply the "Be-Human" rule in dealing with others. In everything you do, show that you put other people first. Give them the kind of treatment you would like to receive.

3. Think progress, believe in progress, and push for progress. Think improvement in everything you do. Think high standards in everything you do.

4. Take time to confer with yourself and tap your supreme thinking power. Use managed solitude to release your thinking power. Set time aside every day just for thinking.

In coaching clients, I find that it helps them when they learn to take time every day to meditate, think, journal, and calm themselves. A regular habit of scheduling quiet time, muscle relaxation, listening to calming music, or even a massage goes a long way in putting them in the right frame of mind. It helps them grow more confident, more relaxed, more sure of themselves; they become BIGGER!

The best individuals to coach are those who are future oriented because that is what inspires them. They talk about their past only in terms of lessons learned. Don't be part of the status quo; stand for progress and take responsibility for the future you create.

IF YOU LEAD THEM THEY WILL FOLLOW

When I left my last real job (one that pays you every two weeks) over seven and one-half years ago, some fellow employees came to my office to wish me well. They expressed the usual well wishes: "good luck," "we will miss you," "it won't be the same without you," etc.

A couple of employees came up to me and said four words that had a powerful impact. These four words have stayed in my mind all these years. They were "take me with you." They wanted to go with me to my next job. They did not know where I was going; I didn't either, and yet they wanted to be a part of my next team, my next venture. Their words resonated with me. What had I done to deserve such a wonderful compliment?

We can all earn the respect of individuals we work with if we demonstrate leadership and show we respect them and care about them. It is a simple concept, yet so many people in positions of leadership fail to act in ways that unleash the power of their employees.

It begins by putting faith in people. When you put trust in people they do things you, and sometimes they, did not know they could do. If you give them the flexibility and train them well, they will rise to the occasion every time, wanting to contribute to the success of the organization.

It is also important that you support them. Sure, they will make mistakes, but if you support the individuals and allow them to learn from their mistakes, they will try new and innovative things without fear of repercussion. If they are afraid to make decisions, it will not benefit them or your organization. Indecision causes more stress in individuals, leading to missed opportunities.

Leadership is not easy. It takes consistent action over a sustained period, especially if you go into an organization where the employees have been neglected, ridiculed, and disrespected. Before they come out from under their desks—or more importantly, their minds come out of hiding—you have to convince them you mean what you say. They have to believe they can hold you accountable. Turning an organization around is not something you can do on a dime. It is not like turning a jet ski; it is more like turning a luxury liner. It is a slow, steady process.

Part of the turning around process is giving positive and constructive feedback. You have to recognize the wrong just as you recognize the right. Not everything goes right all of the time. It is important to acknowledge defeat when it occurs, but just as important to acknowledge the fact that you will survive. Of course if there are too many defeats, that is a different matter. This is a time when coaching should be considered because knowing how to give feedback is crucial.

Organizations are in constant change, so the leadership process is never over. Massimo Ferragamo, Chairman of Ferragamo, USA, said, "If someone says that the changes are over, they are over. I personally believe that every arrival point is a departing point, and you have to always think that way."

When you trust employees, when you give them the opportunity to show their strengths, their spirit will triumph. You will build a team based on trust because they know that everyone contributes, that they count, and that you have their back. If you show you care, they will care.

Leading an organization is a team sport. Smart athletes know that. No matter how skilled an athlete, the smart ones know they cannot do it all by themselves. That does not mean they do not sometimes put the game on their shoulders when needed, but they choose the team over themselves.

Leadership is about taking people with you. You cannot delegate it; it is your responsibility.

Take care, and remember, if I can help you or other leaders in your organization reach their full potential, give me the opportunity.

HOW DO YOU DEAL WITH AMBIGUITY?

The word "ambiguous" has its origins in the early 1520's. It comes from the Latin word "*imbiguus*," which means, "having double meaning, shifting, changeable, and doubtful." Does this sound like some of people you've been around or have worked with? People who are ambiguous are typically not comfortable with change or uncertainty. They may prefer more data, or prefer things tacked down and secure. They may be quick to close and have a strong need to finish everything. Sometimes they do things the same way over and over.

According to studies, 90 percent of the problems of middle managers and above are *ambiguous*—meaning the problem and the solution are unclear. If we had 100 percent of the information, we could make decisions that are more accurate every time. Given the information we do have, the challenge is to make more good decisions than bad ones. We are challenged to do this with less than all the information, in less time, and with little or no precedent.

Dealing with ambiguity is a leadership skill. It's about improving our clarity in dealing with those we influence. There are remedies for overcoming and improving this competency. A chapter in the book *FYI, For Your Improvement*, by Michael M. Lombardo and Robert W. Eichinger, gives us some steps to take when dealing with ambiguity; here are five of them:

1. Take small incremental steps. Many times, we are overwhelmed and lack all the information we wish we had so we shoot in the dark. If we make a series of small decisions, get feedback on them, correct our course of action, and get

more data, we are then able to move forward little by little until the bigger problem is under control. Sometimes the second or third try gives us a better understanding of the underlying issues. Starting small will help us recover quickly.

2. Ask the right questions. Get a firm handle on the problem. Keep asking "why" and go deeper with each question. Before you can focus on the solution, you need to figure out what caused the problem. Defining the problem with the right questions first will lead to better decisions. Focusing on solutions first will slow us down.

3. Manage your stress. As things become less ambiguous, we become stressed. Stress will lead to frustration and cause us to lose our emotional anchor. Think of what causes you to become anxious and study which situations lead to stress. This will enable you to become more aware as a situation approaches, giving you time to head it off. If you need to, let the problem go for a while. Step away from it by doing something else, and then come back to it later. You may gain a new perspective.

4. Don't be afraid to let go. Sometimes you just have to let go. For a short amount of time, you have to hold on to nothing but air, trusting that you will find something to grab. You will land in a new place. The worst fear for many people is change, which is about letting go. Visualize a better outcome, a better place, and experiment. The more you do this the more comfortable you will be.

5. Redefine your progress. You will never finish some projects and tasks. Deal with it. We are constantly editing our actions and decisions. Not everything comes in neatly wrapped packages, which means we constantly have to work in ambiguity, sometimes even abandoning our tasks. The goal should be progress, not perfection. We have to feel good about fixing our mistakes and moving forward.

The world is not clearly defined. Think of it as the path to adventure and a motivator to gain knowledge and understanding. The more you understand what causes ambiguity and how it affects decision-making, the more effective a leader you will be. It is the effective leader who shows confidence and optimism by transforming the unknown into a vision of clarity.

Does this newsletter appear ambiguous, vague, and unclear? If so, don't fret; I don't want it to be too clear, or else you might stop growing.

EFFECTIVE COMMUNICATION REDUCES WORKPLACE STRESS

One of the contributing factors of workplace stress is ineffective communication. It is true. We may not realize it, but the way we communicate is one of the chief causes of stress-related problems. Consequently, one of the ways to reduce uncertainty in the workplace is to improve our communication skills.

Stress is defined by control. Having control over a situation can reduce your stress, while losing control will cause stress levels to go up. We all know that some level of stress can be good. As our stress levels increase, so can our productivity. Positive stress is known as "eustress," a healthy form of stress that keeps us motivated and excited. The opposite of eustress is "distress." Distress has negative implications. Too much of it can lead to exhaustion, illness, and even a breakdown.

Some stress will always be there; it is unavoidable, but we can learn to cope with it better. One way is to get a better understanding of our goals and expectations. Better communication can help. What is important is that we understand and are understood. How many times can you think of when poor communication led to confusion, mistrust, misunderstandings, ill feelings, hurt, false hopes, and even war?

Communicating is not just about verbal expression; it is also about having strong listening skills. It is a two way street, and the way you communicate determines what others think of you as well as how you are accepted and appreciated.

All of us want to be understood; it is one of our strongest desires. We want to have others understand what we think, feel, value, love, fear, and believe. It is not just about speaking or writing clearly, it is about the ability to hear **AND** understand the intentions of every communication. It is also about communicating your intended message successfully. The person listening must interpret your message in the way it was intended. This takes listening skills, something most managers do not give much thought.

The highest form of listening is "empathic" listening. Empathic listening means you understand people from their perspective. It does not mean you accept what they are saying, just that you understand it. You have to develop a frame of mind that is curious; this increases your capacity to listen. In *The 7 Habits of Highly Effective People,* Stephen Covey wrote, "Most people do not listen with the intent to understand; they listen with the intent to reply."

Being a good listener means you have to stop talking and listen. It means you do not think about other things, and that you avoid distractions. It also means that you do not start forming an opinion or start thinking of an answer or rebuttal before the speaker finishes delivering his message. To do this you have to involve all your senses and skills to understand the person.

Empathic listening means you have to listen with yours ears, eyes, and heart. You listen for feeling and meaning. Your verbal message has to be sent and received with the appropriate and corresponding non-verbal message. You will be sending confusing messages if your verbal message is saying no while your head is nodding yes.

In his book *iLead*, Joseph Sherren mentions how we can improve our communications by doing the following:

1. Tune the world out and tune the speaker in
2. Put people at ease
3. Get people to talk about themselves
4. Do not ask threatening questions
5. Make and hold eye contact
6. Listen to how people feel

The last point, "listening to how people feel," is one of the most intriguing. You can listen to how people feel by paying close attention to their rate of speech, vocal variety, tone of voice, and the pitch in their voice. It takes practice, but it can be a very effective listening skill.

Effective Communication is one of the modules in my upcoming **Ascending Leader's Program**™. In fact, it is the longest module (two hours) because I think it is one of the most critical skills a manager, project director, or ascending leader can possess.

THRIVE OR DIE ON YOUR COMPANY'S CULTURE

Organizational culture has been defined as "the specific collection of values and norms that are shared by people and groups in an organization, and that control the way they interact with each other and with outside stakeholders and/or customers."

Organizations can have strong cultures or weak cultures. An organization with a strong culture operates like a well-oiled machine, cruising along with a strong set of values and norms that actively guide the way it operates. Organizations with weak cultures have little alignment with organizational values, and controls are exercised through extensive procedures and bureaucracy.

An unhealthy culture can inhibit growth and even contribute to the organization's eventual failure. In many cases, employees perform only the minimal necessary tasks without putting in extra effort. Productivity and service decline while growth comes to a halt. If entrepreneurs don't see the signals and fail to act, it may be too late to make needed changes. Sometimes failure comes by way of a slow business death.

Some of the warning signs of an unhealthy organizational culture include increased turnover, difficulty hiring talented people, people coming in late to work, lack of attendance at company events, and an "us-versus-them" mentality between employees and management.

In contrast, a strong culture can contribute significantly to a business, but is particularly important to a small business. Culture affects many areas of a company's operations, helping determine its overall ethics and attitude toward public service. It can increase employees' commitment and productivity.

It's not easy to build a strong culture; it takes commitment and hard work. Shawn Parr, an expert blogger, mentions some of the basic things that should be considered.

1. Dynamic and engaged leadership
2. Living values
3. Responsibility and accountability
4. Celebrating success and failure

Yet since every company is different, there are different ways to develop a culture that works. Additional things to be considered include:

1. The prevailing culture should begin at the top.
2. All employees should be treated equally.
3. Hiring decisions should reflect desired company culture.
4. Two-way communication is essential.

Some of the companies with expert corporate cultures are Zappos, Google, Virgin, Whole Foods, and Southwest Airlines.

If you are not investing time in building a strong company culture, then you may not be getting the best from your employees. Instead, you may be hindering the growth of your company.

Coaching and organizational development programs can help identify weaknesses in your company while developing a vibrant culture.

WHAT'S THE FOCUS OF YOUR DAILY ROUTINE?

Many executives and business owners tend to focus on the day-to-day operations of the organization, forgetting to take the time to look in the mirror to reflect on what behaviors they have developed and what changes they can make to improve their overall well-being and performance. They sometimes find that they have stopped growing in their roles and struggle to get help for their own self-development. Sometimes they have been successful and need to take on larger challenges or roles. Other times they simply need a sounding board or someone to help them hone their skills in the talent they already have.

Whether you're in a new role and facing challenges, or are an experienced executive or business owner, coaching can help you change your thinking and behavior. A coach can help you reshape how you see and approach things. Being more flexible and responsive to your circumstances rather than being stuck to habits and patterns can unlock your potential for growth.

Many individuals confuse coaching with consulting. Nothing can be further from the truth. A consultant provides answers to clients, and in most cases, time does the work for them. Then they go away until the client once again needs answers and work done for them. A coach will help the client reshape their thinking and approach, enabling them to be more responsive in formulating answers to their challenges. Coaching is a partnership that is designed to increase work performance, self-management skills, and the ability to effectively manage other people.

If a coaching client is willing to engage in the coaching process, and is committed to learning and growing, a coach can help transition their management skills and leadership style for personal excellence and business success.

Here are just a few reasons why an individual may want to consider the services of a coach:

1. Need to clarify a vision and communicate it so others will follow.
2. Tend to try to do everything themself and don't know how to delegate.
3. Procrastinate due to insecurity because of inner voices (Gremlins) that keep telling them they will not succeed.
4. Lack focus or are over-focused.
5. Struggle with professional relationships and the need to "fix" behaviors.
6. Ready to take the next step and prepare for a larger role and responsibility.
7. Need an unbiased sounding board and/or a need to be held accountable.
8. Know what to do but don't have the tools to implement change.
9. Need to find balance in life and start enjoying the things they love to do.
10. Focused on small details when they should be looking at the "sky-view" of things.

These are but a few of the reasons a person may want to engage the services of a coach. If you see one or more of these in yourself or your valued employees, I might be able to help.

The coaching process can be accomplished one-on-one or as a team or group. With today's technology, we can coach clients located in other cities or countries, without the coach or client ever leaving the comfort of their office.

Become the most effective leader you can be and leave the mindset of "a hope and a prayer" that things will work themselves out. By the time you realize they won't, it can be too late. Coaching is about improvement and changes so that you and your business perform at a much higher level. A coach can be the catalyst to generate that improvement and positive change.

WHAT WILL PEOPLE SAY ABOUT YOU WHEN YOU LEAVE THE ROOM?

What's really important about the work you do? At the end of the day, how do you want others to remember you? Not everyone wants to leave a legacy, and not everyone gives it consideration. However, in reality, the question is not whether or not you are leaving a legacy but what kind of legacy you will leave. What is a legacy and what can you do to leave a positive one.

Your legacy is simply the total sum of the difference you make in people's lives. It's not always obvious; it can be direct or indirect, formal or informal. You won't always know the impact you have on other people's lives. You certainly don't sit and wonder about your legacy or base your decisions on questions such as "What will this decision do for my legacy?"

A positive legacy doesn't just happen; you have to work at it by influencing those around you with your words and actions. These actions may include standing for what is right and taking a risk with quiet tenacity. They may also include being a good teacher and remembering that everyone has to learn and grow. Being approachable and creating a safe and positive environment in your workplace are other actions that build legacies.

It certainly requires being a visionary and charting a course for the future. You influence those around you through the way you live, the words you speak, and the actions you take in your daily life.

Do you believe you're leaving a legacy? If you answered no, then think again—because we are all creating and leaving a legacy. The question is not <u>if</u> you will leave a legacy the question is what <u>kind</u> of legacy you will leave.

Here are three key things you can do to create a positive legacy.
1. Maintain a positive attitude.
2. Be persistent and make the extra effort.
3. Look in the mirror.

Yes, the mirror. You need to look in the mirror of your life to see if you are striving to improve and make sure you are living up to your ability and expectations. It's important to ask your spouse, close friends, executive coach, and trusted colleagues what they see regularly. The answers will not always be what you want to hear because you don't always make the right calls. But if you accept the feedback in the sincere manner it is given, consider it a gift. Without the mirrors, you probably won't receive it at all.

It's not complicated to get that feedback. Simply ask, "How am I doing?" Then sit back and listen without interrupting and without arguing. This is a time to sit quietly and just listen deeply.

You might be the rainmaker in your organization. You might be a brilliant strategist, the best salesperson, the one who drives in all the business, but if you quit or disappeared today, what would you leave behind? Would those who were around you think about things differently or would they emulate what you were doing? Would they say, "I'm never going to do that/be that/or act like him/her?"

It's not about being popular or liked. It's more about being respected. When you treat people with dignity and respect, when you support them, recognize them for the work they do, make them feel wanted and valuable, help them build their skills, and show your confidence in them, it will make your job—and their job—easier. It will help create a lasting positive legacy.

The way that people think, behave, and approach work and life as a result of having known you is the legacy you leave. It has little to do with your abilities, how well you performed your job, or how smart you were. It has everything to do with you, the person at work and in life. It has everything to do with your natural you, not your title or responsibilities. You are the custodian of the future, and it's up to you to make sure you leave things in better shape than you found them.

WHAT IS THE CULTURE OF YOUR ORGANIZATION?

An organization's culture guides the way employees and employee groups interact with one another as well as with clients and customers. But what is organizational culture and why is it important? The topic of this month's newsletter may open your eyes to your organization's internal capacity to sustain itself into the future.

Organizational culture is comprised of attitudes, experiences, beliefs, and values. It is the way individuals and groups interact with each other and other parties they come into contact with outside the organization.

Culture is not something you can see, yet it surrounds you at all times. It is an element that shapes your work enjoyment, your work relationships, and your work processes. It is like personality, made up of values, beliefs, underlying assumptions, interests, experiences, habits, and personal behavior. It is a set of unspoken and unwritten rules for working together.

Organizational cultures are created, maintained, or transformed by employees or leaders. Typically, it's the leaders who establish the parameters, the values, and norms of the organization's culture.

The organizational culture is made up of all the experiences each employee brings to the organization. It is in the language, decision-making, symbols, dress codes, stories, legends, and work practices. It is in the company newsletter, bulletin boards, meeting interactions, and the way people collaborate.

Cultural characteristics come into play as a company or organization tries to determine if a candidate is a "good fit" as an employee. It's hard to define, but sometimes the person doing the hiring can just tell that it "feels right" when making a hiring decision.

Organizational culture consists of three levels: behavior and artifacts, values, and assumptions and beliefs. To understand culture we must understand all three levels.

Many leaders try to shape or reshape their organization's culture when starting a new company. Others take this approach when the organization is not performing at peak levels. Cultural change strategies can be implemented to improve organization or company performance.

Culture may not necessarily be defined as good or bad, although it can have an effect on the success of an organization. It can be the norm whether it is spectacular customer service or tolerating poor performance. Sometimes the first contact helps others shape an opinion of your organizational culture.

While it can be a premier advantage for high-performance companies, it can be difficult to change. Culture develops and affects the way in which an organization responds to its internal and external environments. Many times defensive actions hinder and sabotage the organizational system, sometimes unwittingly.

What's your organization's culture?

CAN EMOTIONAL INTELLIGENCE MAKE US SMARTER THAN INTELLECT ALONE?

To the ancient Romans, *"sensus communis"* meant common sense, humanity, and sensibility, which included the full use of the senses, the heart, and intuition. Today's business runs on brainpower, but to compete effectively it must incorporate another important aspect of intelligence often left untapped. This additional resource is better known as "emotion," the vastly overlooked fuel that drives the brain's higher reasoning power. In many workplaces today, productive workers are thwarted or sabotaged by the lack of, or gaps in, emotional intelligence within themselves, their bosses, or others around them.

People can be successful in their chosen profession if they learn the importance of emotional intelligence and allow it to play a role in maximizing emotional and social functioning. It has been demonstrated that those with higher Emotional Intelligence (EI) are more likely to perform at higher levels than their less emotionally intelligent peers or co-workers.

We can improve our emotional intelligence through training and assessments. Research has also shown that emotional intelligence can predict effective transformational leadership skills and leadership performance.

However, in order to improve our emotional skills and abilities, we have to recognize our strengths and those areas that require improvement. The Emotional Intelligence Skills Assessment (EISA) is one program that measures these strengths and areas for improvement.

The five EISA factors are:

1. Perceiving
2. Managing
3. Decision-making
4. Achieving
5. Influencing

Perceiving emotion is the ability to accurately recognize, attend to, and understand emotion. Having the ability to perceive information about other people starts with being aware of emotional signals, accurately identifying and defining them, and applying them to a given situation.

Managing emotions is the ability to manage, control, and express emotions effectively. It is a skill that allows us to evaluate and adequately control our emotions in order to function effectively.

Decision-making using emotion is the appropriate application to manage, change, and solve problems. The appraisal of our emotions affects the intensity of our mood and can influence our thoughts and behaviors.

Achieving emotion is the ability to generate the necessary emotions to self-motivate in the pursuit of realistic, meaningful objectives. People who use their emotions to achieve their goals are often motivated to succeed and spend less emotional energy and time thinking about failure.

Influencing emotion is the ability to recognize, manage, and evoke emotion within oneself and others to promote change. Emotions can play a role in creating and maintaining social relationships. This can be evident in our capacity to evoke emotions in other people.

Each of the five factors above can be developed or improved upon to maximize one's performance. Taking an Emotional Intelligence Skill Assessment can provide insight into your level of professional emotional and social functioning.

The EISA is an assessment tool I am incorporating into my coaching programs for my clients. With feedback from managers, peers, direct reports and others, the assessment can be used to understand one's own emotions, stay abreast of the emotions of others, demonstrate empathy, and illustrate the difference between emotions. We then use developmental exercises to improve EI skills and develop a goal-setting plan.

Those who use emotional intelligence in their workplace and their personal lives can identify skills they can rely on during times of heightened stress. They can also identify areas for improvement. The appropriate use of your emotional intelligence can significantly improve your job performance.

DOES BEING IN A POSITION OF LEADERSHIP MAKE YOU A LEADER?

Now that the election is over, we can settle into a more normal routine without the constant bombardment of negative ads, false accusations, and hyperbole. Regardless of your political affiliation, you have to ask yourself if the elected officials actually possess the skills and traits required to call themselves leaders. Being in a position of leadership does not make them leaders.

Being in a position of leadership is a responsibility they should not take lightly. Individuals should step into their leadership role with compassion and a responsibility for others, **all others**, not just those affiliated with one party or another. Isn't this a radical idea these days, to be a leader for all the people, regardless of their political affiliation, color of their skin, or religious beliefs?

That's right, religious beliefs. Religion has become a factor in the political process. It's scary how the more we send our troops to fight for freedom in the Middle East, the more we behave like a Middle Eastern country. Don't think it's true? Just look at how religion has become embedded in our political process. Consider the anger and hate it generates among candidates and constituency groups as well.

Civility has left our political process, and there are few, if any, elected officials who have the willpower to demonstrate effective leadership. It's not hard to do; anyone can be a leader, regardless of where they are in an organization or elected body. Leadership is not about a position; it's about demonstrating leadership traits.

Many individuals don't consciously prepare themselves for leadership. Perhaps they are born with some leadership qualities, or they model someone, learn it from leadership programs, or consciously have the self-discipline to become an effective leader. For some people it's all of the above. I have worked for some very effective leaders and some ineffective ones (don't ask me for names of the ineffective ones). The effective leaders demonstrated the key characteristics people look for in a leader: **honesty**, **forward-looking**, **inspiring** and **competence**.

John Maxwell, author of *Developing the Leader Within You,* writes about the five levels of leadership.

1. Position – People follow you because they have to.
2. Permission – People follow you because they want to.
3. Production – People follow you because of what you have done for the organization.
4. People Development – People follow you because of what you have done for them.
5. Personhood – People follow you because of who you are and what you represent.

Too many politicians are leaders by position. Wouldn't it be nice if they would strive to become leaders by personhood?

Individuals in a position of leadership have a tremendous amount of influence, and that's something they should not take lightly. They should develop great teams, develop others, understand basic human needs, select good people, show compassion, know what is required of them, keep improving, and communicate effectively. Most important, they have to accept final responsibility.

Leadership development is important in politics and in business, no matter the size of the organization. If your company or organization has one hundred employees, one inferior employee is a loss of one percent. If it has two employees, one inferior employee is a loss of 50 percent. If you are a sole proprietor, your business could be 100 percent inferior. Don't make the mistake of thinking that you can get by with inferior leadership because you are in a large organization or don't need leadership development because you own a small business.

I offer you and your employees the opportunity to enhance your leadership skills. The **Ascending Leader's Program™** is developed to assist those you value. When you can't hire the best, hire those who can become the best. Then give them the leadership tools they need to excel.

WHAT IS THE GREATEST GIFT YOU CAN GIVE YOURSELF?

I tell my friends and clients that it's not bad to be self-employed, if you have a good boss. That has to be one of the best advantages of being self-employed, along with being able to resolve staff conflicts quickly, never disappointing your co-workers when arriving late or leaving early, and being able to put an end to office gossip.

Of course, there are some drawbacks. When you arrive at the office in a foul mood, the entire workforce is affected. Plus carpooling or calling in sick is definitely out of the question.

One of the highlights of being self-employed is fast approaching, the Christmas gift exchange between employees. I always seem to know what type of gift I would like. And not surprisingly, I always seem to receive it. My employee has great insight.

Having received some great gifts during my self-employed lifetime, I started thinking about the best. It didn't take long to choose one from the many. Easily the best gift I have received is also the wisest for business. It is the gift of *personal development.*
Investing in self-improvement, in my own personal growth, in the betterment of *me* is the best gift I have ever received. It is, without a doubt, the most critical step in accomplishing my goals. It's also the one on which all success strategies are built.

Abraham Lincoln said, "Give me six hours to chop down a tree, and I will spend the first four hours sharpening the axe." In other words, he would spend twice as much time working on himself as on the task itself.

Most people would grab the ax, dull or not, and start chopping the tree. If they don't make any progress, they quit—and probably blame the axe. Their best strategies and actions, how hard they hit the tree, their rhythm, etc., can all be measured and improved—but the work starts with the axe itself. We are the ax.

If we accept that professional development is important for us, then we should also agree that professional development is important for our employees. Why not give your employees the gift that keeps on giving? Give them the gift of personal development.

If personal development can make you a better leader, it will make your employees better leaders, better managers, better supervisors, better co-workers, and better members of the community. Everybody wins when that happens.

Sir Ernest Shackleton, the great Antarctic explorer, believed that a good boss can make the workload seem lighter, that not providing our workforce with the best tools available unduly burdens them, and that one person can affect the entire workforce. Providing opportunities for personal development creates a workforce that can help your organization grow.

The holiday season is a time for giving; why not give your employees the gift of personal development? You will be giving them something that will last a lifetime. Investing in their personal development will improve awareness and identity, develop talents and potential, build human capital, enhance quality of life at home and at work, and contribute to the realization of their dreams and aspirations. You will be helping them reach their potential, and that will help you reach yours.

AUTHENTIC LEADERSHIP

When developing leadership skills, individuals will often identify leaders with characteristics they wish to emulate. They focus on leadership styles rather than character. Yet regardless of your leadership style or the type of leader you are, it is important that you develop a persona or authenticity that is consistent with your personality and character.

Developing your leadership style is something that takes time and hard work. Authentic leaders are not born authentic. Unlike some who are born with natural talent, they must develop themselves into true leaders—ones with passion and compassion.

Developing as a leader means accepting your faults as well as your strengths. When people become too eager to win approval, they may sacrifice their authenticity while trying to mask their weaknesses. Or they might succumb to the pressure to succeed and lose sight of their core values.

In an article on authentic leadership, Bill George, a professor of management practice at the Harvard Business School, writes about the essential dimensions of all authentic leaders. They are:

1. **Understanding your purpose:** You find your purpose by understanding yourself, your passion, and your underlying motivations.

2. **Practicing solid values:** Your values are shaped by your personal beliefs and your experience. Your values define your moral compass; but for

sure, integrity is one of the values required of authentic leaders.

3. **Leading with heart**: Successful leaders engage the hearts of their employees. This means being open and willing to share as well as taking a genuine interest in them.

4. **Establishing close and enduring relationships:** Developing close and enduring relationships are essential. It lets your employees know you're interested in their success and are concerned about their careers.

5. **Demonstrating self-discipline:** This means demonstrating your values, and when you fall short, admitting your mistakes.

Watching my clients develop their leadership skills is one of the most rewarding parts of my job. They use their natural abilities and work hard at overcoming their shortcomings. They know their values, and people know where they stand. They are focused, consistent, self-disciplined, and refuse to compromise their principles.

Sometimes it's like watching an acorn grow into a magnificent oak tree.

www.ingramcontent.com/pod-product-compliance
Lightning Source LLC
Chambersburg PA
CBHW032307210326
41520CB00047B/2274